Hidden by Darkness
Kim Taylor

Delacorte
Press

Published by Delacorte Press
Bantam Doubleday Dell Publishing Group, Inc.
666 Fifth Avenue, New York, New York 10103
This work was first published in Great Britain
in 1990 by Belitha Press Limited.
Text copyright © Kim Taylor 1990
Photographs copyright © Kim Taylor and
Jane Burton 1990
Consultant: Ellen Fader

Manufactured in Great Britain
September 1990
10 9 8 7 6 5 4 3 2 1

**Library of Congress Cataloguing-in-Publication
Data**

Taylor, Kim.
  Hidden by darkness/Kim Taylor.
    p. cm. – (Secret worlds)
  Summary: Describes animals which are active
at night, such as the cockroach, bat, and
nightjar.
  ISBN 0-385-30178-2.
  ISBN 0-385-30179-0   (lib. bdg.).
  1. Nocturnal animals – Juvenile literature.
[1. Nocturnal animals.] I. Title. II. Series:
Taylor Kim. Secret worlds.
QL755.5.T38   1990
591.5 – dc20   89-78287
                                           CIP
                                            AC

_A_ S THE SUN SETS, THE FULL MOON RISES AND NIGHT begins. All sorts of things happen in the dark, but they are difficult to see because our eyes only work properly when there is plenty of light. At dusk, everything looks blue; this is because most of the light comes from the sky, which is blue. But, as night descends, the sky turns inky black and the trees and fields are lit only by the moon. Then blue things look pale, and red things look black. But the colors _are_ there all the time as this photograph of holly berries taken by moonlight shows. After all, moonlight is just sunlight reflected off the surface of the moon.

Creatures of the night

MOTHS FLY AT NIGHT. SOME, LIKE THIS MALE DRINKER moth, have feathery antennas. It uses its antennae to smell, and is so good at it that it can smell a female drinker moth more than a mile away. Moths can see to fly when the moon is shining, but on dark nights, they often fly toward street lamps or lighted windows. Some caterpillars are active at night, too. These elephant hawk moth caterpillars hide close to the ground during the day. Now that it is dark, they have climbed the willowherb and are looking for leaves to eat.

Cockroaches live in food stores, kitchens, and even in drains. When the lights are turned off at night, they crawl out from cracks and crannies to eat crumbs of food. If the light is turned on again, they quickly scuttle away. Close up, a cockroach is really quite beautiful, as this picture (*below left*) shows. The green oak bushcricket is also a beautiful animal with fine lacy wings. It has just hit its head on an acorn as it came in to land. The night-time calls of the male oak bushcrickets are so high-pitched and faint that only other oak bushcrickets can hear them.

Night noises

SHEARWATERS ARE SEA BIRDS THAT NEST IN UNDER-ground burrows on remote islands. Each female lays only one egg. One parent sits on the egg while the other goes fishing far out to sea—for three or four days. Thousands of fishing birds return to the island at night and fly around in the darkness making eerie cackling noises. Each sitting bird recognizes the voice of its mate and answers from its burrow. If you stand among the shearwater burrows on a really dark night, you may feel a soft, feathery thump as a flying bird crashes into you. Shearwaters cannot see very well in the dark.

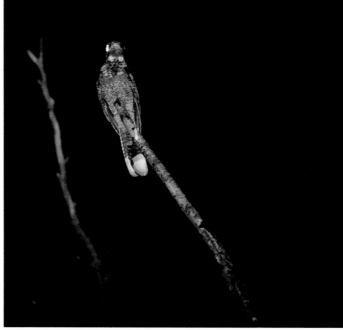

The forests of Africa are very noisy at night. Loud creaking noises followed by creepy-sounding screams echo through the swaying trees. These sounds are the calls of tree hyraxes, furry animals that look a bit like rabbits. At night the hyraxes come out from holes in the trees to munch leaves and scream at each other.

Another strange night noise is the purring of a nightjar. It sounds very much like a purring cat except that it is louder and goes on and on and on.

Tree frogs (*above left*) gather near ponds in spring where the males make a terrible noise, *crack, crack, crack* . . . From a distance, crowds of tree frogs sound like quacking ducks.

Reed frogs, like this African one (*above right*), live close to lakes and marshes where they, too, make a lot of noise. This one has blown up his throat into a balloon and is saying loudly, *Pinkle!* When walking at night in the African bush, you know that you are coming to a swamp when you hear the *pinkle, pinkle, pinkle* of hundreds of reed frogs in the distance.

Eyes in the dark

CATS SLEEP A LOT DURING THE DAY AND WHEN THEY open their eyes in sunlight, the pupils are just little slits. At dusk, when a cat goes hunting, its pupils open fully so that as much of the dim light as possible can get into its eyes. This is how cats can see so well in the dark. If you hold a flashlight close to your head and shine it at a cat, you will see how its eyes reflect light. Most cats' eyes reflect green or blue, but cats with eyes that are blue in daylight, like the one above, reflect red at night-time.

Echoes in a cave

*B*ATS OFTEN LIVE IN CAVES WHERE IT IS DARK ALL THE time and come out only at night, so you rarely see them. There are two kinds of bat; insect-eating bats, which have tiny eyes, and fruit bats (*like the one above left*), which have huge eyes and can see in the dark. Their eyes reflect like cats' eyes (*above right*). Here you are looking up at the roof of a large cave where hundreds of glowing-eyed fruit bats are hanging upside down. The noise of twittering and fluttering bats is deafening.

Insect-eating bats, like the leaf-nosed bat (*below left*), cannot see in the dark. They find their way by squeaking and listening for the echoes. That is why they have big ears. Their eyes are just like little beads and not much use. Other kinds of animals, like these cave fish (*below right*) have been living in darkness for so many thousands of years that their eyes have just about disappeared. Even with almost no eyes, cave fish can swim around without bumping into anything. They can *feel* the echoes of tiny pressure waves in the water as they swim and these tell them when a rock is close by.

Big ears

*L*ONG-EARED BATS FLY AT NIGHT AMONG THE TREES. Their squeaks are so high-pitched that you cannot hear them. As it flies, each bat squeaks all the time, listening for the echoes that tell it how close it is to the trees. At the same time, the bat is listening for the sounds of an insect that will make a tasty meal. The bat's ears are huge and can hear the tiny scrape of an insect's feet as it walks across a leaf or the soft purring of a moth's wings as it gets ready to fly away.

Cold dew

DEW FORMS DURING THE NIGHT. YOU CAN SOMETIMES feel a little dew on the grass soon after sunset but, by morning, there are drops on every blade. Even flowers, like this rose, and sleeping insects, like this dragonfly, become coated in dew. Where does dew come from? It doesn't fall from the sky like rain, since the heaviest dew forms when there are no clouds. Dew comes from the air itself. As the ground cools on a clear night, dampness in the air condenses onto plants and other things to form dew. Clouds are like a blanket; they keep the ground warm so that dew does not form.

Web work

SPIDERS CANNOT SEE IN THE DARK, BUT THEY BUILD their webs at night when they are safe from hungry birds. They are able to work in the dark because they can feel their way with their feet. They can tell by pulling gently on a strand of web that it is attached at the other end, and they know just how tight to pull it to make a support for the web. Spiders build webs to catch flying insects, but on cool nights they catch dew (*above left*) and on windy days they catch blowing seeds (*opposite*). Most spiders live alone but when a thin male and a fat female meet, there is often a battle (*above right*).

Listening in the dark

OWLS HAVE BIG EYES AND CAN SEE IN THE DARK. THEY also have very good ears. The barn owl (*above*) is taking off for a night's hunting. As it glides over the fields, it is listening for little rustling sounds made·by mice in the grass. Its feathers are very soft so that they make no noise in flight and the mice cannot hear it coming. The owl pounces on a rustle and may not know what it has caught until it pulls its victim out from under the grass. The little owl (*opposite*) is *not* a baby but a grown up and very keen beetle hunter.

Town mice and country mice

*D*EER MICE (*ABOVE*) LIVE IN THE COUNTRY AND ARE VERY good at climbing. They use their tails to help them balance as they run along thin twigs. These mice have found some peanuts meant for the birds. They carry the peanuts away, one at a time, and store them. They may empty the whole peanut holder in one night. House mice, like the ones opposite, live in towns. They have become very good at stealing food from kitchens and storage places during the night. They have even learned to live in refrigerated warehouses where they grow shaggy coats to keep themselves warm.

A slow crawl

SNAILS NEED MOISTURE TO MAKE SLIME, AND THEY cannot crawl without slime. So, when the weather is dry, they just stay in their shells. But at night, when dew forms, they come out of hiding to eat leaves. If you get up very early on a nice day you may see snails here and there but, soon after sunrise, they all will disappear. You *can* see the slime trails they leave behind. In fact, one snail is late getting home and is hurrying to get there before the sun becomes too hot.

Index